A Kid's Guide to

Origami ™

Making
ORIGAMI
VEHICLES
Step by Step

Michael G. LaFosse

The Rosen Publishing Group's
PowerKids Press™
New York

To the memory of my father, Gerard LaFosse

Published in 2002 by The Rosen Publishing Group, Inc.
29 East 21st Street, New York, NY 10010

First Edition

Book Design: Emily Muschinske

Project Editors: Jennifer Landau, Jason Moring, and Jennifer Quasha

Illustration Credits: Michael G. LaFosse

Photographs by Adriana Skura, background image of paper crane on each page © CORBIS.

    LaFosse, Michael G.
    Making origami vehicles step by step / Michael G. LaFosse.
       p. cm.
    Includes bibliographical references and index.
     ISBN 0-8239-5875-2
    1. Origami—Juvenile literature. [1. Origami. 2. Handicraft.] I. Title.
    TT870 .L23424 2002
    736'.982—dc21

                                                       00-013048

Manufactured in the United States of America

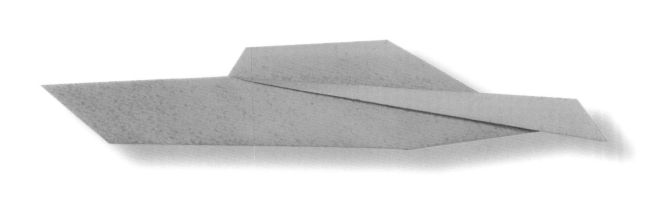

Contents

What Is Origami?

In Japanese, "ori" means folding and "kami" means paper. That is why the Japanese art of paper folding is called origami. Origami has been popular in Japan for hundreds of years. Today people all over the world practice the art of paper folding.

Like music, origami uses a special language of **symbols**. Once you know the "language" of origami, you can read an origami book from any country, even from Japan!

All of the origami in this book is folded from square paper. Most origami paper has color only on one side. You do not need to buy special paper, however. You can make origami using magazines, notepapers, or wrapping paper. Make sure that the paper you use is square. It should also be the proper size for your project. A few origami projects in this book use more than one sheet of paper. The Airplane and the Truck are two such projects. These two-piece models let you mix and match different colors of paper in one model. The key on page 22 will help you make your origami projects. The key explains terms such as <u>mountain fold</u> that are used throughout the book.

Submarine

Vehicles are used to carry people and things. The submarine is a special vehicle that allows people to explore the world's oceans. Although boats and ships can travel on top of the water, storms can make this dangerous. The submarine allows people to travel deep beneath the stormy sea. When you travel on a boat, you must bring food and fresh water. When you travel on a submarine, you also need to bring fresh air or a way to **purify** the air you breathe. Submarines can be large or small. Some are only big enough to hold one person. Some are used to study animals that live only in the deepest parts of the oceans.

1

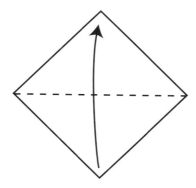

Use a square piece of paper 10 inches (25.4 cm) wide or less. If you are using origami paper, start with the white side up. Fold in half, from one corner to the other.

2

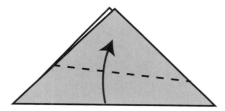

Fold up the bottom edge of the paper. Make one end lower than the other. The low end is the back of the submarine.

3

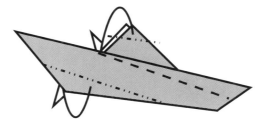

Fold down the back corner. Then fold the top and bottom corners to the back.

Space Shuttle

A space shuttle rides a rocket to get above the **atmosphere** where there are no clouds or air. It is sometimes used to carry people and equipment to a space station, and sometimes to bring **satellites** into **orbit**. A space shuttle can be used to visit an orbiting telescope to service or repair it. Like a submarine, a space shuttle must hold all the food, water, and air that a crew will need. When a space shuttle lands, it glides to Earth without power. The bottom of the space shuttle gets very hot when it contacts the atmosphere at high speed. The bottom is covered with special tiles that protect the shuttle from very high heat.

1

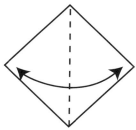

Use a square piece of paper 10 inches (25.4 cm) wide or less. If you are using origami paper, start with the white side up. Fold the paper in half, corner to corner, then unfold it.

2

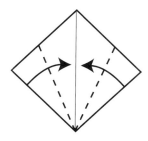

Carefully fold two edges to the crease to make a kite shape.

3

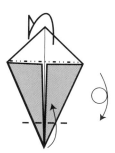

Fold up a little of the bottom corner, then fold down the top corner to the back. Turn over the paper.

4

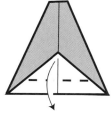

Fold down the top of the triangle so that it falls below the bottom edge of the paper.

5

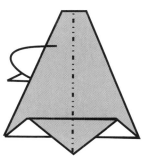

Fold in half, making sure that the triangle of paper is on the outside of the shape.

6

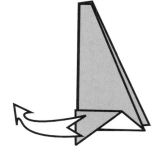

Pull the triangle to make it stand out like the tail of an aircraft. Press the paper hard to make it stay in place.

7

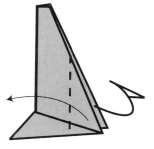

Fold out the wings, one on each side.

Airplane

It is fun to **invent** new paper airplanes. More than 150 different **designs** have been invented. Most of the paper airplanes that have been designed are made by folding only one piece of paper, but this two-piece design flies so well and is so simple that it may become one of your favorites.

After you have folded this Airplane and flown it, you may be surprised to find that if you pull the "nose" from underneath, the airplane turns into an elephant! Either way you will enjoy this design, and it really flies well.

1

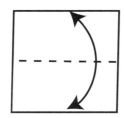

Use two square pieces of paper 6 inches (15.2 cm) wide or less. Smaller models fly the best. Fold one piece in half, edge to edge, and unfold.

2

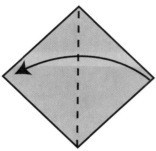

Fold the other piece of paper in half, corner to corner, to make a triangle.

3

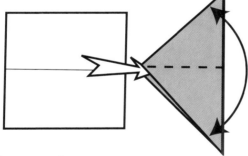

Fold the triangle in half, corner to corner, and unfold. Slip the other paper inside the triangle, making sure to line up the creases.

4

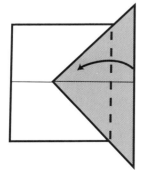

Fold over the long edge of the triangle.

5

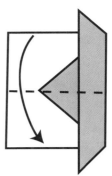

Fold in half, wing to wing.

6

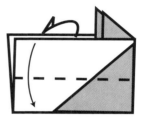

Fold down the wings, one on each side. Open the wings and throw!

Jet

Here is another two-piece paper airplane design. Like the first airplane design, this plane has more layers in the front, thanks to the extra piece of paper. This added weight in front helps carry the paper airplane farther, just as a rock goes farther than a cotton ball when thrown. This Jet is as sleek and trim as a dart. It should travel fast if folded neatly. Real jet airplanes also must be sleek and trim because they often travel very fast. A jet's engines burn fuel, which releases energy as the fuel is combined with oxygen from the air. A jet cannot travel into space because space has no oxygen.

1

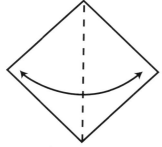

Use two square pieces of paper 6 inches (15.2 cm) wide or less. Fold the first piece in half, corner to corner, and unfold.

2

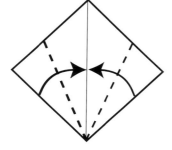

Carefully fold two edges to the crease to make a kite shape.

3

Fold up the bottom point. Make it cover the two paper corners.

4

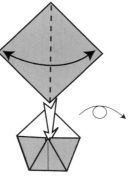

Neatly fold the second paper in half, corner to corner, and unfold. Slip this paper inside the first, making sure to line up the creases. Turn over the paper.

5

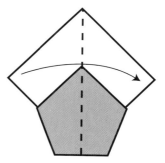

Fold the paper in half, wing to wing.

6

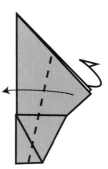

Fold down the wings, one on each side.

7

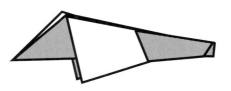

Open the wings and throw!

Truck

A truck is a vehicle that is designed to carry large or heavy objects. Using trucks is an **efficient** way to move things around the country. Some trucks carry fresh food and are like refrigerators on wheels. We can have fresh fruits and vegetables even in the winter because these items are brought by truck from warmer **climates** to colder areas.

This origami Truck is made from two pieces of paper. One piece is the vehicle and the other piece is the load. You can change the size or color of the load. You can even write or draw on the load to show what your Truck is carrying.

1

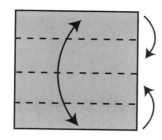

Use two square pieces of paper 10 inches (25.4 cm) wide or less. If you are using origami paper, start with the colored side up. Fold the first paper in half, bottom edge to top edge, and unfold. Fold the top and bottom edges to the crease.

2

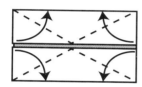

Fold out the four corners.

3

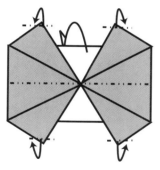

Fold a little of each of the four corners to the back, then <u>mountain fold</u> in half.

4

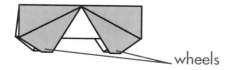

The paper should look like this.

5

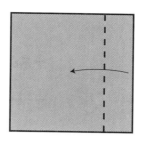

Fold in the right edge of the second paper.

6

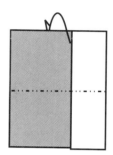

<u>Mountain fold</u> in half.

7

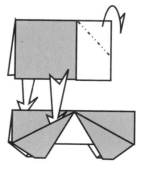

Fold back the right corner. Insert this second paper into the first, one edge on each side and behind the wheels.

Car

Cars come in many shapes and sizes. There are fast cars for racing, and there are big cars that can carry many people. The word "car" is the short form of the word "**carriage**." Carriages used to be pulled by horses. The first cars were called horseless carriages. Many of them were powered by electricity. Today most cars run on gasoline, which is a fuel that uses oxygen. There are also some new designs for cars powered by electricity once again.

1

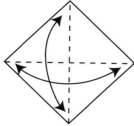

Use two square pieces of paper 10 inches (25.4 cm) wide or less. If you are using origami paper, start with the white side up for the first piece of paper and the colored side up for the second. Fold the first paper in half, corner to corner, both ways. Unfold each time.

2

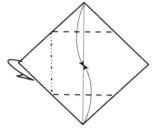

Fold in the top and bottom corners. <u>Mountain fold</u> the left corner. All three corners should touch the center creases where they cross.

3

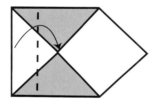

Fold over the left edge.

4

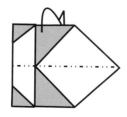

<u>Mountain fold</u> in half.

5

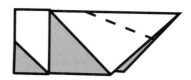

Fold over a little of the point.

6

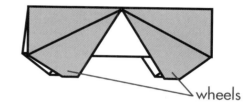

wheels

With the second piece of paper, follow steps 1–4 on page 15 for making a truck.

7

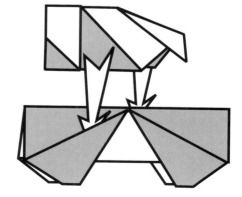

Insert this second piece of paper into the first, one edge on each side and behind the wheels.

Sailboat

Sailboats move through the water best when the sailor moves the sail perfectly. The sailor steers the boat using sails and a rudder, a movable blade that sticks into the water. The sailor holds a rope to bring the sail closer to the center of the boat, or to let it out farther. The front sail is sometimes called the jib. The rear sail is sometimes larger, and often is called the mainsail. This origami Sailboat is fun to sail along a smooth tabletop. You can have races with your friends' boats. Blow gently enough to move the boat without tipping it over.

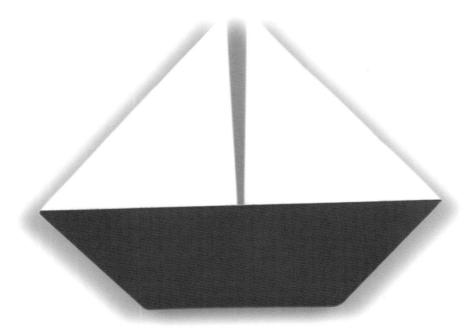

1

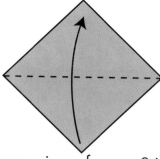

Use a square piece of paper 8 inches (20.3 cm) wide or less. If you are using origami paper, start with the colored side up. Fold in half, corner to corner, to make a triangle.

2

Fold up the left and right corners to meet at the top. Unfold.

3

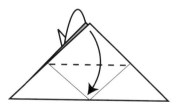

Fold down the two top corners, one to the front and one to the back.

4

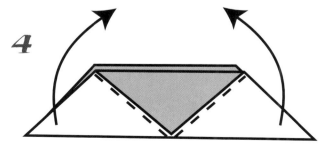

Fold up the left and right corners.

5

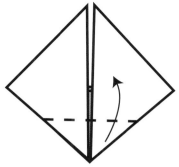

Fold up the bottom corner so that the tip touches the center of the paper.

6

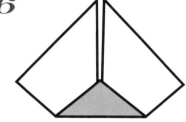

Turn over the paper.

Sailboat Envelope

An envelope is also a kind of vehicle. It carries a message. Envelopes travel all over the world with the help of trucks, trains, boats, and airplanes. An envelope is a vehicle that you can use to send something special to someone in another part of the world. Although you can call people on the telephone, or e-mail them your message using a computer, these messages are not as personal or as **unique** as a letter mailed in an envelope you made yourself. This clever design holds itself together without glue or tape. You can make this Sailboat Envelope as large or as small as you need. Now you can send your best wishes to a friend by way of a Sailboat!

1

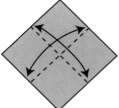

Use a square piece of paper 8 inches (20.3 cm) wide or more. If you are using origami paper, start with the colored side up. Fold in half, edge to edge, both ways to make crossing creases.

2

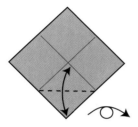

Carefully fold the bottom corner to the center where the creases cross. Unfold. Turn over the paper.

3

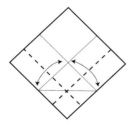

Fold the bottom right edge to the crease, then unfold. Repeat with the bottom left edge.

4

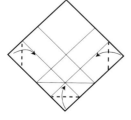

Fold up the bottom corner to touch the crossing creases. Fold in the left and right corners to line up with their creases.

5

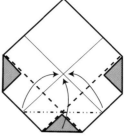

Fold up the bottom edge. At the same time, fold in the left and the right edges. Make each end of the <u>mountain fold</u> meet at the center of the paper. Look at the next picture to see what the paper should look like.

6

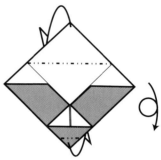

<u>Mountain fold</u> the top and the bottom corners to the back. Turn over the paper.

7

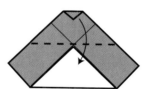

Fold down the top edge. Make the paper fold at the top of the white triangle. Put your letter or card behind the white triangle when using this envelope.

8

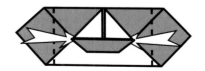

Fold in the sides and tuck them behind the sailboat. The envelope locks itself closed!

Origami Key

1. MOUNTAIN FOLD

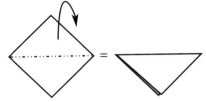

mountain-
fold line

To make a mountain fold, hold the paper so the bottom (white) side is facing up. Fold the top corner back (away from you) to meet the bottom corner.

2. VALLEY FOLD

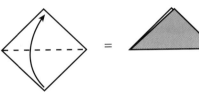

valley-
fold line

To make a valley fold, hold the paper so the white side is facing up. Fold the bottom corner up to meet the top corner.

3. TURNOVER

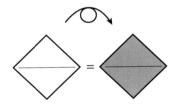

4. ROTATE

 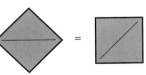

5. MOVE or PUSH

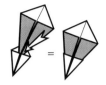

6. CUT

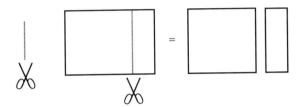

7. FOLD and UNFOLD

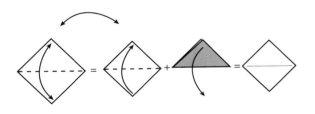

8. DIRECTION ARROW

Glossary

atmosphere (AT-muh-sfeer) The layer of gases that surrounds an object in space. On Earth, this layer is air.

carriage (KAR-ij) A wheeled object used to carry people or things.

climates (KLY-mits) The kinds of weather certain areas have.

designs (dih-ZYNZ) Decorative patterns.

efficient (ih-FIH-shent) Done in the quickest, best way possible.

invent (in-VENT) To design or create something new.

orbit (OR-bit) A path that circles around something, especially a planet, moon, or star.

purify (PYUR-ih-fy) To make pure or clean.

satellites (SA-til-yts) Spacecrafts that move in orbits around Earth, the moon, or other bodies in space.

symbols (SIM-bulz) Objects or designs that stand for something else.

unique (yoo-NEEK) One of a kind.

Index

A
Airplane, 4, 10
atmosphere, 8

C
Car, 16
carriage, 16

D
designs, 10

J
Japanese, 4
Jet, 12
jib, 18

M
mainsail, 18
mountain fold, 5

O
orbit, 8

R
rudder, 18

S
Sailboat, 18
Sailboat Envelope,
    20
satellites, 8

Space Shuttle, 8
Submarine, 6
symbols, 4

T
Truck, 4, 14

Web Sites

To find out more about origami, check out these Web sites:
www.origamido.com
www.origami-usa.org